DIVINE WEALTH STRATEGIES

BOOST YOUR FINANCIAL IQ AND REFRAME YOUR MINDSET

Authored By: **Arpita Mishra**

Terms and Conditions

Table Of Content 💡

Foreword

It's so crucial to set your financial priorities in life as this may help secure your financial future. Too much stress could come from mishandled funds.

A lot of individuals have no idea precisely where or how they spend a good portion of their income. How many times have you taken money from the ATM only to realize a few days later that it's gone? Many times, it's hard to remember how precisely you spent the money, and frequently this money is wasted on frivolous buys.

A budget will help avoid this by making an individual accountable for the income that they spend. If an individual only has $50 left for monthly food expenses then they might decide to give up purchasing that fancy $3 designer cup of coffee.

Well, while you enjoy your cup of coffee, enjoy this book!

Best,

Arpita

That's me, as soon as I finished writing the "Divine Wealth Strategies"!

Chapter 1: ♀

What are My Priorities and Financial Position?

Scrutinize of your financial wellness! As well get your priorities straight.

Some individuals might make mistakes in setting their financial priorities like saving more for their children's college education and a lesser for their own retirement.

The Start Point

♀   What major fiscal challenges do you face?

♀   State your financial positives in terms of revenue, debt management, and savings.

♀   How do you think you arrived at this point—and what would you like to see altered?

♀   How well organized are you for a financial emergency? Write it out now: The amount we have put away an emergency fund is _____.

♀   How is the subject of money addressed in your family: emotionally or rationally?

♀   Who makes the fiscal decisions? How come? How much collaboration is there?

Why it counts: Clarity and commitment. Authorities agree that before crunching the numbers, families need to scrutinize their financial wellness—and the best chance of success comes from having both mates on board.

Here we will explain to you the basic principle of personal financial ratio and its analyses. This will help you keep a tab on your personal finances. Now what are personal finance ratios, you'd ask.

As the name hints these ratios deal with your personal riches, assets or cash in hand. All the more they're exceedingly simple to understand. Just plain discipline of sustaining a budget and statement of assets (what you earn or have) and liabilities (what you spend or what you owe to other people) will help you check your financial wellness.

Here is an easy guide which will help you to comprehend these ratios in detail. Let us have a look as to how these ratios may help.

Basic solvency ratio

This ratio signals your power to meet monthly expenses in case of any emergency or calamity. It's calculated by dividing the near-term cash you have with your monthly expenses.

Basic solvency ratio = Cash / Monthly expenses (this ratio isn't mentioned in percentage). You are able to also call it as emergency or contingency preparation ratio. This ratio helps you prepare for unexpected troubles.

An illustration, a 30-year-old businessman whose wife had an emergency gall bladder surgery last year. In spite of the fact that they had enough insurance to take care of exactly such an event, due to a few administrative problems on the day of discharge, he was informed that he would have to pay in cash as the bill couldn't be settled.

He had a hard time arranging the funds on an emergency fundament. He was fortunate to have good acquaintances and relatives who lent him the money. But not everyone has such great admirers or relatives to bail them out at such short notice. I'm sure no one wants to be in the same shoes.

Therefore, we have to be organized for such a situation. How? By sustaining an emergency fund!

Let's examine how much money is adequate. Here is where basic solvency ratio comes handy.

The numerator of the basic solvency ratio formula, cash (near cash), would commonly comprise of the following things:

- Savings account
- Bank fixed deposits
- Liquid funds
- Cash on hand

The above elements are liquid assets which come on handy at the first hint of financial problems. Liquid funds may be delivered immediately. Same goes for fixed deposits as they may be broken and liquidated at once in case of an emergency.

Monthly expenses:

Only the mandatory fixed and varying expenses are taken here for ease. Any amusement outlay shouldn't be taken as these expenses can be quashed.

Mandatory fixed expenses include the income you pay for, loans, insurance premium, and rent.

Mandatory varying expenses, on the other hand, comprise of food, transit, clothing/ personal care, medical care, utilities, education expenses and assorted compulsory expenses (the above expenses can vary depending upon individuals).

The total of the above divided by 12 (that is 12 months) helps you attain the monthly average as your variable expenditure might change. Assuming that you've cash of 60,000 and median monthly expenses of 25,000 your basic solvency ratio would work out to: 60,000 / 25,000 = 2.4.

But is it great?

Not quite. An Ideal ratio should come to 3.

What does the number 3 mean?

It means that you must have money equal to or at least 3 months of your mandatory expenses in a contingence or emergency fund.

How come just 3 months? This is because research shows that 3 months' time is enough to emerge from any type of financial pinch. As individuals near their retirement age, they should make certain that this fund is kept up to six months of their required expenses. The fund should be divided and kept in the form of cash, fixed deposit, or liquid fund.

You should understand how to prioritize your financial goals so that you'll stay pleased and financially stable as you get older in life. This doesn't mean that you don't consider the future of your kids but you're just setting your financial priorities in order.

Set an amount monthly for food, water and shelter as these are your primary needs. You need to think about buying various healthy foods and attempt to avoid unneeded snacks that are unhealthy. You likewise need to do your best in your present job as it's your source of income to pay for your utility bills, home mortgage or rent, and groceries. This is where you start setting your priorities straight.

A few individuals are so frugal on their grocery shopping, they disregard their health needs just to buy expensive gadgets or airplane tickets for a leisure time. Observe that attending to your own daily needs is your duty and priority to prevent evading the rent or house mortgage, utilities and other crucial matters for well-being particularly if you have a family.

Occasionally this could be the cause of disagreement between man and wife for they've different views when it comes to income management. The other mate wants to spend most of the money and isn't afraid of financial debt while the other one prefers to save something for the rainy days or an emergency. Be a good role model to your youngsters as they think highly of you as a parent.

Pay your credit card debt if you have any. Paying-off the credit card with the highest rate of interest then followed by the ones with lower rates of interest is the best thing that you can do in order to eradicate your entire credit card debt. Purchase things or goods with cash as much as possible and contain your spending habits.

Prevent over using your credit card so that you'll be able to continue to have access to your accounts if you truly need it. Some individuals, who were working and never bothered to save for an emergency fund and over used their credit, now have nothing. You don't want to be in a spot where you've no earnings and can't even access your credit cards because your accounts are closed.

Center on saving enough cash for your emergency fund particularly when all of your credit card debt is paid-off. This is really crucial in case of a job loss or other major unforeseen things that might happen to you or anybody in your family. Avoid the enticement of purchasing things that you are able to just live without and center on building your emergency savings.

Setting your financial priorities should be your principal ambition. Have a clear list of the crucial things that will cover your monthly expenses and finances and number each item from the highest to the lowest with regards to their importance and need.

Step-up your 401(k) or a 403(b) contribution and retirement savings if you already have enough cash savings for your emergency fund. Try to save 15%-20% of your salary for retirement.

Try to save for your retirement before saving for your youngsters' college education. When your youngsters grow up, they can use student loans, get scholarships or attend a good community college or state university where it's more affordable. As you consider their future, you likewise need to think of your golden years.

Capitalize on free training opportunities. Attending free seminars and trainings to advance your knowledge is a very good investment for your future. Setting career goals in life is really crucial as the job market is highly competitive.

Revise or update your will to make certain that your wishes are secure and accomplished. You need to have estate planning regardless how small your estate is. Some individuals will just assume that their assets and possessions will automatically pass to their family but without a legal will, the State might step-in and allocate your property or estate.

Valuate your insurance coverage. Check whether your car and homeowner policies are updated and their deductibles are fair. You might seek life insurance particularly if you're the head of the family working full-time. You may likewise think about buying long-term-care insurance, to aid you in paying for nursing care or assisted-living when you get old.

Chapter 2: 💡

Where Does All My "Greens" Go?

Perhaps you thought you knew how much you spent on mega lattes, till you saw the numbers in front of you. For most individuals there is $65-$85 a month in savings or more than $750 a year. Leave out Starbucks and eating out every day.

Take a look at non-monthly bills, like car insurance, vehicle registration... decide between needs and wants.

Important Info

In today's domain there are very few individuals who take the time to produce a personal budget. Some individuals don't see the value in doing so; others merely have no desire to confine their spending habits.

With this in mind, it should surprise no one that the number of personal bankruptcies has achieved an all time high. Individuals have achieved a point in our society where they purchase on impulse with no thoughts to the outcomes.

In order to reverse this trend, individuals need to become more responsible with their forms of spending. Among the best tools to help a person achieve this conduct is the personal budget.

A personal budget is a financial plan which sets bounds on the sum of money that will be spent on each category of expenses in a given month. A beneficial budget will take into consideration such elements as: the amount of income being obtained, owed debt to be retired, retirement savings, and an emergency fund.

A benefit of a budget depicts an accurate idea of how much a person can actually afford to pay for assorted consumer items. Whether it's a home, a car, or a new TV set, an individual will be able to ascertain whether or not a particular purchase will fit within their monetary constraints. This acts as a precaution against getting in over your head financially.

It's crucial to realize that merely creating a budget isn't enough. This in and of itself will do an individual absolutely no good if he doesn't discipline himself to stick to it.

Occasionally this will very hard, especially if an individual has founded the habit of freely spending without an afterthought. However, the long-run advantages of financial freedom, debt free living, and a comfortable retirement far outbalance any potential difficulty.

List as many of these bills as you are able to identify over a 12-month period.

Now, employ the "one-twelfth" rule, where you put aside funds for these expenses monthly, so as to limit their impact when payments come due.

Next, center on where you are able to spend less money without depriving yourself.

- What uneconomical or indulgent practices can you cut down on? (Cab rides when you are able to walk, expensive lunches.)

- Do you often shop for items you don't require?

- Are you paying too much for services like car insurance, cable or cell phone service?

- Do you have unused memberships (e.g. gym) that you're still paying for (and may sell)?

It's easy to distinguish between the two if you go by a textbook definition. But actually, the distinction is hard and has been getting narrower over the past few years.

Nowadays, a car has become an emotional need in spite of the existence of an efficient public transport system. The need for an auto has transformed from a status symbol to a luxury to a basic essential now. The same system of logic applies to food.

From home food to a fast food joint, nowadays buyers expect a fine dining experience and not just good food. This ambience comes at a premium and individuals just don't mind paying for it.

The truth is, wants are inexhaustible and often the lines between needs and wants get blurred. Therefore, one needs to get into self-examination before giving into the impulse to splurge.

Let's presume a family of 4 spends $8,000 on food, $25,000 on shelter, $20,000 on education and $10,000 on transportation. Now calculate the difference between your outlay and earnings. All you have to do is to write the primary price list and the cost of living in your city and compare the areas to give you a truthful picture.

If you require a mobile because you've a field job, it's a need. But if you insist on the latest gadget which you are able to truly afford, it's a want. That was an easy pick. But it gets hard if you have to trade off an automatic washer for a refrigerator or substitute a radio with a home theatre-com-music system. Think about it!

Chapter 3: 💡

Pay Yourself FIRST!

Odds are fantabulous that once you tweak and streamline your budget, you'll have some breathing space. What's the first thing you should do with any freed-up cash? Authorities agree unanimously: Make saving a top priority, even if you have debts.

The average American with a credit file is responsible for $16,635 in debt, barring mortgages. Presume that the annual percentage rate for interest on that deficit equals ten percent, and you're paying $200 a month. Assuming you don't score any more debt, you won't be in the clear for twelve years.

The great news: you are able to dig out sooner if you stand by some easy guidelines.

As you break the excess spending habit, and fall under the savings habit, you're ready to take on the next step: building investments, retirement savings and real property equity. Sound unachievable?

Altering Actions

Among the oldest rules of personal finance is the easy word of advice to pay yourself first. All the money books tell you to do it. All the personal finance blogs say it, too. Even your parents have given you the same advice.

But it's difficult. That money could be used somewhere else. You could pay the telephone bill, could pay down debt, and could buy a new videodisc player. You've tried once or twice in the past, but it's so simple to forget. You don't keep a budget, so when payday comes around; the income just finds its way elsewhere.

To pay yourself first means merely this: Before you pay your bills, before you buy foodstuffs, before you do anything else, allow a portion of your income for savings. Put the income into your 401(k), your Roth IRA, or your savings account. The first bill you pay monthly should be to yourself. This habit, acquired early, may help you build tremendous wealth.

Once you pay yourself first, you're mentally founding saving as a priority. You're telling yourself that you're more important than the light company or the landlord. **Building savings is a potent motivator — it's empowering.**

Paying yourself first furthers sound financial habits. Most individuals spend their money in the following order: bills, fun, saving. Unsurprisingly, there's generally little left over to put in the bank. But if you bump saving to the front — saving, bills, fun — you're able to set the income aside before you justify reasons to spend it.

By paying yourself first, you're constructing a cash buffer with real life applications. Steady contributions are an excellent way to build a savings. You can use the money to deal with emergencies. You can utilize it to purchase a home. You can utilize it to save for retirement. Paying yourself first gives you freedom — it opens a domain of opportunity.

The best way to acquire a saving habit is to make the process as painless as conceivable. Make it automatic. Make it invisible. If you arrange to have the money taken from your paycheck before you get it, you'll never know it's gone.

The true barrier to acquiring this habit is discovering the money to save. Many individuals believe it's impossible. But almost everybody can save at least 1% of their income. That's only one penny out of every dollar. A few will argue that saving this little is non-meaningful. But if a skeptic will attempt to save just 1% of his money, he'll commonly discover the process is painless. Perhaps next he'll try to save 3%. Or 5%. As his saving rate increases, so his savings will grow.

If you're scrambling to find money to save, consider setting aside your next raise for the future. As your income grows, set your gains aside for retirement and savings. Once you're imparting the maximums to your retirement (and you've built emergency savings), you are able to start to utilize your raises for yourself again.

Pay yourself first, my friends. It's a habit that you'll never regret.

Begin keeping really close track of your spending. A number of little comforts in your budget might have to be eliminated in order to make ends meet. Restaurants, cinemas and other expensive entertainment may be substituted with libraries, galleries and outdoor exercise. Papers, magazine subscriptions and cable TV are likewise good candidates for budget cuts. One expenditure that might be worthwhile, however, is a personal finance program that trails your debts, assets and cash flow on a day by day basis, so that you recognize precisely where you stand at all times.

Whatever you do, do not miss a payment. Late payments may truly hurt your credit score, and thus make it even more grueling for you to secure more positive financing. This may affect your insurance rates likewise. Making the lower limit payment by the deadline on your credit card is much brighter than making a larger payment a couple of days late.

A second source of income may make a huge difference to debtors. If you are able to earn just $500 a month extra, that's $6,000 a year that you are able to apply toward debt reduction. Another thought is reducing the amount of tax you've withheld from your check. Having no tax deducted may be advantageous in some cases. Naturally, you'll have to pay the tax with interest and penalty at the end of the year, but these rates are typically much lower than standard credit card rates.

Don't hesitate to get help if you require it. Talk terms with creditors and see if you are able to work out a satisfactory settlement. Credit and financial counseling services may be invaluable resources and might be able to point you to options or tips that you'd never discover otherwise. They may likewise begin you on a debt management or consolidation program to help lower your rates.

Lastly, if all else fails, see if you are able to get a debt consolidation loan from a family member. You are able to offer to pay them a rate that's much lower than your credit card interest, but much higher than what they'd get in a checking or savings account.

Some investment steps to think about:

- Meet with a financial consultant or certified financial planner to view this all-important part of your budgeting.

- Acquire a solid plan and stick with it. All too frequently we've become complacent when the market is doing well and cowardly when the market isn't doing so well. What sets the successful individuals apart is containing those emotions.

How come it matters: development—personally as well as financially. You've got to go from a spendthrift to budgeter, a budgeter to a saver, and a saver to an investor.

Ascertain what items or issues you're saving for. These may be retirement, a new house, your youngster's education or anything else you choose.

Ascertain when you want to retire, buy a house or send your youngsters to college, to help you decide what percentage return you need to earn on your initial investment.

Determine how much money to invest. Invest what you are able to comfortably afford now, keeping in mind that you are able to change that amount later.

Ascertain how much risk you're willing to take. Many investments bring forth high returns and are riskier than others.

When you decide the amount you're willing to invest, the returns you want to accomplish, when you need the money and how much risk you're willing to bear, assemble your investment portfolio.

An investment counselor or stockbroker is a great source of advice. Tell these advisers your objectives and ask them to propose how to allocate your income.

Chapter 4: ♀

There are lots of ways to save at home. On a day when fun is required, but funds have been wiped out, you need to enjoy your life! Believe it or not, the finest things in life are free! The things here will show you how to have fun free of charge, no matter where you are.

Tips!

Save income on electrical energy.

♀ Put in the new type of fluorescent bulbs in lights you leave on for long periods. They provide 4 times as much light and last 10 times longer than incandescent bulbs. **Likely Savings: $10-$50/yr.**

♀ Lower the temperature on your water heater to between 110 and 120 degrees. It's not essential to have it any hotter and wastes energy. **Likely Savings: $20-40/yr.**

♀ Discover if your utility company offers free energy audits, where they audit your home for energy effectiveness and advocate inexpensive ways to cut energy costs, like insulating the water heater, weather-stripping, and so forth. Just insulating your water heater may save you $25 a year. **Likely Savings: $50/yr.**

💡Set thermostats no greater than 68 degrees in winter and no lower than 78 degrees in summertime. Turn your heat down even more at night or when you're not home (unless you've a heat pump, which operates more efficiently at one uniform setting). Each extra degree in wintertime may increase heating costs by 3%. In summertime, each degree may raise cooling costs by 6%. **Likely Savings: $325 to $500/yr.**

💡Cut down on the use of your dryer. Not only is it a huge energy drain, it may also suck heated air out of your home very quickly in wintertime. Hang clothes on a clothes rack to dry out and use the dryer for towels and other heavy items. **Likely Savings: $25-50/yr.**

💡Utilize your microwave rather than your oven if possible and save up to 50% in energy costs for cooking. **Likely Savings: $50/yr.**

Save income on water.

💡 Always do full loads of wash. A typical full load utilizes about 21 gals of water. A little load uses 14 gals. Several small loads utilize substantially more water than one or two big loads. Over the course of a year, this adds up. **Likely Savings: $25-$125/yr.**

💡Run your dish washer only when you've a full load. Let the dishes air-dry rather than utilizing the heat cycle. An average dishwasher costs $60 to $100 annually to run. **Likely Savings: $35-55/yr.**

💡 Mend running toilets or leaking faucets quickly. An endlessly running toilet may utilize more than 8,000 gallons of water a year. **Likely Savings: $25-125/yr.**

💡 Put in flow restricting shower heads. A family of 4 may save 8,000 to 12,000 gals of water a year. You not only save on the cost of the water, but likewise the cost of heating it. **Likely Savings: $100-$300/yr.**

💡 Add fabric softener to your laundry at the suitable point in the cycle rather than adding it at the end and running a different rinse cycle, which may use up to ten extra gals of water. Figure out how much time it takes your washing machine to reach the rinse cycle, and set a timer so you are able to add softener at the right time. **Likely Savings: $25-100/yr.**

💡 Utilize warm or cold water for washing apparel, and always rinse in cold water. **Likely Savings: $50/yr.**

Save money on other.

💡 Use basic phone service. Extra services like call waiting and call forwarding may nearly double your costs for the phone. **Likely Savings: $168/yr.**

💡 If you are able to live without cable, you are able to save between $300 and $600 annually. If you can't live without it, acquire basic service only. You are able to rent a lot of movies for the extra $150 to $600 annually you pay for movie channels like HBO, Showtime, etc. **Likely Savings: $144-700/yr.**

💡 Plant perennial flowers rather than annuals. You receive a one-time cost and enjoy the flowers for a long time, with little additional effort or income. Annuals, on the other hand, call for an outlay of cash and effort yearly. **Likely Savings: $100-$300/yr.**

💡 Head out to the beach! Public beaches are free and amusing. You are able to also walk on the boardwalk. Have fun constructing sandcastles or sport fishing on the pier.

💡 Go window browsing. Go to a strip mall and check up on the fresh arrivals. Just remember that you don't have to confine your window browsing to clothing stores. Stop by the window exhibits at electronics and jewelry stores. Fresh technical gadgets are always appearing on the market!

💡 Ask about free company amenities. You might not know this, but a lot of times the company you work for has a list of places (i.e. museums and aquariums) that are free of charge if you give your work identification card at the admissions counter!

💡 View each season as a fresh way to have fun. In the summertime you are able to shoot hoops at the basketball court, play tennis or walk around the neighborhood with your acquaintances. In the autumn you are able to pull out your camera and take pictures of the fall leaves. Fall is likewise a good time to go to a pumpkin patch. Wintertime is amusing because you are able to play in the snow or remain inside and watch the snow with a cup of hot chocolate or a café latte. Springtime is good for bicycling!

💡 Ask in your friends for a night of board games, cards and charades. The cover charge is a little dish or drink of choice. Your donation will be the free entertainment, so be ready to host!

💡 Stuck at home with the youngsters? Whether they're on vacation from school or visiting for the weekend, here's a couple of great suggestions on how to entertain them free of charge.

💡 Think about going to free community festivals, free movie events and free parks.

💡 Think about a day at the beach, a picnic in the park, hiking in the woods, or a different outdoor activity. Swimming, outdoor games and adventures are an affordable and effective way to spend the day with kids.

💡 Have a rainy-day list of thoughts ready likewise. Visit your local library and rent some kid-friendly films and play "movie theater": have the kids make up tickets, set up the front room like a movie theater and pop some popcorn. You are able to also make up your own board game with novelties around the house, produce drawing and coloring games, or do easy crafts.

💡 Capitalize on ticket upgrades. It may cost a little more at the beginning, but consider year-round passes for local attractions for a good way to spend the day. Your local zoo or aquarium might offer such a deal, as well as funfairs and more.

💡Generally, kids have capital ideas! Just be ready to give them a free or affordable option. For instance, if they suggest going out for ice cream, think about buying ice cream and cones at the food market instead and heading to the park. If they want to go out for pizza pie, purchase grocery items to make a pizza and turn it into an activity alternatively. A good imagination, and willingness to try fresh things, will help you go a long way, and help you stretch your dollar while entertaining youngsters at the same time.

Chapter 5: 💡

Let's Monetize Your Skillset Even When You Have None...
(P.S. – All You Need is English)

Everybody could use some surplus money, especially in hard times. Maybe the bills were a bit more than you'd anticipated this month or perhaps you're attempting to raise some starter cash for your own online startup or business or perhaps you just need to figure out how to ramp up your existing business.

💡 **Make an e-book**: all right, your thought is – everyone and his father are doing this these days. However, why? Because it works. If you're well-educated about a certain topic, e.g., how to weather coat a deck, power wash a house, give up smoking, make doll apparel – whatever it is, author a book about it.

A Bit Extra

Freelancers are a forward-looking lot. All the same, almost every day I get questions from those who find it difficult to make a sustainable living. I ascribe most of this to some people's inability to think differently.

There are a lot of ways to make income as a freelance person that I keep a file of thoughts. While I seldom find myself without a project on my desk, when work gets scarce, I go through this file to perk up the brain cells. Today I'll share the ideas with you.

This might call for a bit of up front work, however may bring in dollars for a long time to come. There are so many web sites in painful need of great copy that all you have to do is switch on your computer to turn one up. All the same, the key is to target those who are willing to compensate for your services.

An acquaintance of mine knows an apothecary who made a skin care product. The product is distributed across the country through independent distributors. My acquaintance told me to check over the site to see if it was a product I'd be interested in trying out.

When I got to the site, I instantly forgot about why I was supposed to be viewing the web site. How come? The grammar, artwork and layout were atrocious; particularly the grammar! I rewrote the home page and sent it off to the webmaster with a courteous note stating that I'd be happy to remake the entire site for $x. Inside a few days we came to terms and I got the job. You are able to do this also.

Professionals are a good target market for freelancers. Mortgage companies, insurance companies, lawn care suppliers, and so forth. Most have sites – and a lot of them are not very good. So, edit/re-script a page and send it to them with a proposition to do the whole web site.

Commonly, if they use you once, they'll continue to do so for years to come. Offer to add each week, each month, every quarter, and etcetera. Add articles to the site to step-up traffic. A lot of small business owners are so busy that they don't think or understand how to do this type of marketing. Call attention to the advantages and watch your customer list grow.

Consider the content for each page. For instance, you are able to go into company history on the "About Us" page, but you can likewise mention that your company has x years of experience on the home page, also. You are able to bullet your services on the home page and then go into detail about them on the "Services" page. Jot down some points for the content of each page. Decide where you want particular tidbits to be highlighted so each page isn't repetitious.

Add a little SEO. Do some research on the net to determine what keywords are "red-hot" for the industry. If the company, for instance, makes kitchen cabinets, you might want to include terms like "kitchen remodeling" "kitchen cabinets" and "kitchen cabinetry" to name some. It's likewise a good idea to provide a regional aspect for individuals seeking the business locally. For instance, "kitchen cabinet maker in AZ" and "kitchen cabinets AZ" are good terms to work into the copy.

Utilize an attention-grabbing headline for each page. Rather than "Cabinet Makers" you may try something like "Distinctive Cabinets for Custom Kitchens." When you get into the "core," remember to talk to your specified audience.

Will you refer to the customer directly? No one truly cares about the content unless it offers them something. Rather than bragging about why the company is the best, or presenting a history of kitchen cabinets it's beneficial to keep in mind that you need to explain the advantages of what the company has to offer. What can Joe Blow get out of the site, and why should he pick this company to build his cabinets?

I always end each page with an easy "call to action." For instance, "Are you ready to discover how you are able to have the kitchen of your dreams? Contact us at (phone) or email us at (e-mail)." You get the idea. The goal is to drive the reader to take action.

Authoring e-books is simple – it may be done in as little as twenty-four hours – and you can offer it for sale on a web site like Click Bank or Commission Junction. Think though, most individuals look to the net for info. And, "how to" info is among the most popular forms.

So, squeeze your brain for what you like to do, author an e-book about it and sell it thru a major distributor like **Click Bank**. One book likely won't make you rich, but it may bring in extra cash for a long time to come. **The most beneficial part about this idea, once you make one e-book, you are able to make others and truly build your income to the point where you are able to quit your awful day job.**

Think about your target audience, your book's advantages to them, its core, and center like a laser on that. It might seem to you that just everybody' will want to read your book - but that idea may make your book too 'generalized'. Remember, if you center your efforts on a particular topic instead of generalizing you'll appeal powerfully to a certain audience and reap more possible sales. It's rather like centering on a puddle rather than an ocean.

Get to Understand your target readers; what troubles might your book resolve for them? Where is your book purchasing audience? Try to author a title that includes your audience in it. If not there, then maybe in the sub-title?

You have to be author and promoter, so write and make your sales info about your book as you author your book. Collect data about yourself for your author blurb (whatever qualifies you to author the book, maybe other publishing credits, any experience that's a plus), write about the advantages your potential purchasers are seeking and are likely to discover in your book. Get a few testimonials.

Check into places like Amazon to see what books are selling well and read their 'blurb' content for thoughts on how to present your own. A visit to your local bookshop is a great idea also. Check into some of the other marketers who are marketing books online. Do an 'E-book' search. How are they marketing?

Author an attention-getting table of contents for your book. Title your chapter and add a sub-title to make it transparent to your reader what is contained inside. Read the table of contents of other authors to get an approximation of what may be 'attention-getting'.

That should get you going. Now, do some net searches, hunt down the needed info to get yourself set in motion, but mind the rip-off artist out to get your money. Subscribe to a few newsletters by individuals who are legit. Think about each step of the process, keep notes and keep acting.

Chapter 6: 💡

The Ugly Truth About Credit Cards and Borrowing

One of the biggest challenges for people to overcome when they first determine to start building wealth and putting income away for their future is a hulking mountain of credit card debt developed over several years. The debt has to be first.

As well, a lot of financial planners will tell you to use a **HELOC**, or home equity line of credit, to pay down high interest credit card debt. **Don't do it.**

See the Debt?

Do you prefer to know the fastest way that somebody still isn't ready to accept responsibility for their own financial life and take charge over their credit card debt? It's that they still blame other people, the economy, the economic system, form of government, their boss, or anybody or anything other than themselves.

The only justifiable and logical excuse is those unfortunate persons who find themselves in the middle of a horrifying health scare and rack up monumental debts to make it. Unless that's you, there is something you need to find out: Cut It Out.

You're not a foul person. You are not a stupid individual. You just made a few dopey choices. It had nothing to do with your revenue. It had nothing to do with your loved ones. Every time you used your credit card, you made a conscious decision to borrow what you did not have. The very beginning month the statement showed up and you could not pay off the total balance in full, you had surpassed your resources. That's the minute you got in trouble.

This subject matter should not be discouraging! Rather, it should empower you. If you got yourself into immense credit card debt then you have the might to get yourself out of it. It's that easy. The moment you are able to look into the mirror and state, "it's my fault" and sincerely own the situation, you are able to start to turn it around just like 1,000,000s of individuals before you have done.

Take back your power. Discover a symbol of what you feel on the inside or the self-confidence that you want to show to other people on the outside. Having a symbol of what you're thinking or striving for is key to gain assurance. To get to the finish line or get any goal, you need to know where you're going. Your symbol may be anything from a color that makes you feel mighty or an event in your life that really made you feel powerful.

Make a treaty with yourself to always put yourself first. The fight to gain self-assurance is often derailed because individuals tend to put the needs of others before their own. You need to put yourself first in your life if you really want to gain any ground in your life.

Place your best foot forward day-after-day if you want to know the true secret of how to gain authority. It's a shown fact that individuals who put out what they believe to be their best outfits and do their hair and makeup in a way like they were going out on a special night on the town, feel more potent in themselves. Bet you didn't know that the easy task of putting on a shirt that you save for "special occasions" on a regular day will help you to gain assurance more than any self-help guru could ever.

Take back your self-power and take responsibility.

Several individuals that I know are in significant credit card debt and sometimes ask my thoughts on how to get out of the state of affairs. While I'm happy to spend time assisting them, it almost always turns out to be a senseless exercise as in 90% of the cases, the individual isn't truly serious about getting out of credit card debt. Sure, they're miserable about the payments and the thing they wish for more than anything else is that their credit card statements showed a $0 balance. Wishing for something and doing something to proactively have it are two totally different matters.

Someone I know (I'll call Tom) makes approximately $85,000 annually and has $20,000 in credit card debt. This debt is sweeping over like the plague and he spends at any rate a couple of hours daily nervous over the $500+ per month in interest payments it takes just to sustain his current balance. Yet, at any rate once a month, he discovers $100 to go on a weekend trip. **When I ask him about it, he states that there are particular things that he won't abandon regardless how bad the debt is.**

Tom may never get out of credit card debt with a mental attitude like that. The extra $1,200 annually that he's spending on the weekend getaways would pay down $6,000 of principal over 5 years, or nearly 40% of the balance. If he could make an extra $50 per week either by working a lot of hours or cutting costs (yes, this virtually means you get on a bicycle rather than driving), he may pay off an extra $11,000 in principal over those same 5 years. That's all it would take to wipe out the balance.

Rather, he thinks in terms of "my vacation money" or "my food market money". No, you have one, jumbo pile of money that's available to you. If you're in credit card debt, paying monumental interest on your balances, take every extra penny you are able to and pay down the debt.

Set a sum monthly for food, water and shelter as these are your primary needs. You need to think about buying assorted healthy foods and attempt to avoid unnecessary snacks. You likewise need to do your best at work as it's your source of income to pay for your bills. This is where you start setting your priorities true and right.

Some individuals have their priorities so messed up they even ignore their health just to buy expensive gadgets or

travel. Observe that taking care of your own every day needs is your responsibility and priority so avert putting off the important things particularly if you have a family.

Pay your credit card debt. Paying-off the credit card with the highest rate of interest then followed by the ones with lower rates of interest is the most beneficial thing that you can do in order to wipe out your entire credit card debt. Buy things with cash as much as conceivable and control your spending.

Center on saving enough cash for your emergency fund too. This is really significant in case of a job loss or other major unforeseen matters that might happen to you. Ward off the enticement of purchasing things that you are able to just live without and center on building your emergency savings.

Adjusting your financial priorities should be your chief concern. Have a clear list of the crucial things that will cover your monthly disbursements and finances and number each item from the highest to the lowest with relation to their importance and need.

I'm not a huge fan of home equity lines for one easy reason – if you do decide to utilize the nuclear option and declare bankruptcy, your credit card balances are un-guaranteed, while a home equity line of credit is guaranteed by your house.

Practically, this means that you've taken a debt supported only by your credit, where the worst a credit card company can do is go to court and get a judgment against you, into a debt supported by your house, where the worst is far more awful – the bank may foreclose on your house and kick you out.

No matter, this is entirely your call as it's going to come down to what will let you rest at night. If your credit card debt is manageable, and you just prefer to save a couple of thousand dollars in interest expense, a home equity line of credit may add up. If you think there's even the remote possibility that you might be forced to declare bankruptcy, it may be a tragic mistake that costs you your home.

There are a lot of credit lenders out there today wanting you to put up the equity in your home to get their money for almost any reason you might determine. Among the ways you are able to claim the equity in your house from lenders are by refinancing, securing a second mortgage, a home equity loan, and a home equity line of credit. Are utilizing these ways to borrow money to ease debt a good idea? Here are some good reasons why you shouldn't use equity in your home to pay off debts:

If you get in a financial tie up, and you feel like you have to default on your new secured debts, the fresh debtors may start foreclosure proceedings to get paid as the house is a secured interest. Creditors who make un-guaranteed loans like credit cards can't foreclose on your home as their loans are not guaranteed by home equity.

Even in a few areas of a down market, your home might be appreciating in value. That means your equity is increasing with time. When you borrow against your equity to pay for debts, you'll lose the appreciation the house has amassed if your home is foreclosed on. You will not only owe the guaranteed loan amount, but many times the sale of foreclosed property sells for cents on the dollar. Consequently, the equity you were forecasting to pay off the fresh secured loans won't be there to pay them off.

Getting into debt appears to be a symptom of a much deeper issue.

Using your equity to pay off debts is no guarantee that new debts won't happen. If new debts occur and you've liquidated the only asset you have to the point it already belongs to somebody else, you've increased your debt load to the place you might not be able to afford.

So, what should you do to avoid the temptation of borrowing against the equity in your house? You are able to learn to live within your means, stay out of debt as much as conceivable, pay as you go, look for employment that's resistant to economic shifts, stand back from high interest loans like credit cards if you have to borrow money, and ultimately, keep yourself educated as to the legalities and financial responsibilities that go along with home ownership.

Chapter 7:

One strategy for reducing credit card debt suggested by financial planners is to freeze your cards in blocks of ice, helping you avoid the enticement of inessential purchases.

Find a way to bring in some extra money.

In the domain of personal finance, the "big red button", the atomic option, is taking bankruptcy.

Dig Out

A long time ago, a financial planner told customers to freeze their credit cards in blocks of ice. When they were enticed to spend, they would be forced to dissolve the ice, giving them time to take a second thought about an impulse purchase.

An even more beneficial answer is to cut up your cards totally so that you cannot charge anything else to them. What good does it do to stop up holes in your boat in you are perpetually drilling fresh ones in the side?

Some people may be thinking...But I cannot pay my bills without a credit card! That means that I do not get to eat.

This might sound cruel, but I have news for you: you are not paying your bills really. The credit card is simply allowing you to put off the crack of doom and helping to guarantee that when it does come, it will be much worse than you ever thought.

If you are correct, you will almost sure as shooting qualify for free food assistance in your state (if you do not, move to a state where you do – I'm being serious). In a few states, you are able to get up to three hundred or four hundred dollars per month in tax-exempt food money on a debit card. If you do not qualify, then you have a spending issue and you are still making justifications (go back to chapter 1).

If you still state you cannot make due: you really are full of it. Once again, my apologies, but it's straight up.

I knew someone else who decided she would like to get herself out of debt. She decided that inside one year, she was going to have paid back totally everything in her life, down to the spick-and-span new car she had bought recently.

She went and got a job as a bartender on top of her day job, pitting away every cent after taxes and utilizing it to pay down the outstanding balances on her accounts. She temporarily put all investing on hold, including retirement shares, to accomplish the goal she had determined she would accomplish.

What she has accomplished in short order has been absolutely astonishing. With six months to go, it appears that she is going to easily get to her goal. By bringing in more money into the equation, she was able to blend cost savings from her regular job (she as well did away with her cellular phone, cable, and a lot of other unneeded items) to have double the effect.

Once this self-imposed financial diet is all over, her monthly revenue will go up by as much as several thousand dollars without a single supplementary hour of work. In effect, she gave herself a pay raise. In spite of raising her youngsters and working two jobs, she likewise recently enrolled in college to go back and acquire her degree.

The point of this story is a mighty one. There is absolutely nothing you cannot achieve if you center yourself and are willing to take on the sacrifice necessary to accomplish it.

In her case, that's going to mean a year of around-the-clock work to give herself a fresh balance sheet and more beneficial job opportunities. A long time from now, I am willing to bet that she will look back and recognize that this twelve-month period was what allowed her to go after her bigger goals and dreams, which include establishing her very own business.

As the old saying goes, till the pain of staying the same surpasses the pain of change, you're unlikely to move. I hope it doesn't take that for you to get empowered and free yourself from financial slavery.

Credit card companies, many of which are possessed by banks, have a lot of priorities. The first, naturally, is to yield profit for the parent company and its shareowners (you might actually be a shareholder through the mutual funds you hold in a 401(k) account without even recognizing it).

When it becomes evident that somebody might be unable to pay his or her balance, there's a priority shift that happens that may work to your advantage. The bank or credit card company becomes concerned with one matter and one matter only: **Getting as much of the balance back from you as conceivable and closing or restricting your account.** How come? This lets them avoid charging off the amount on their earnings report, which would cause their stock to fall, management to get lower bonuses, and maybe even dividend payments to stockholders to be reduced.

If you declare bankruptcy, it's possible that the entire credit balance will be annihilated because credit card debt is called unsecured in most all cases. That means that it isn't backed up by any specific collateral, just your promise to repay. This would be the worst-case scenario for the credit card company.

If you've missed a lot of payments already and your credit score has been hit, all it takes is a series of calls to the company explaining that you are earnestly considering bankruptcy but you want to avoid that. You would like to make good on as much debt as you are able to but, frankly, you don't know if it's conceivable. Then, offer to pay off 25%

of your credit card debt balance over the next few months in exchange for the company freezing interest costs and closing the account.

You might have to spend several hours, or even days, on the phone working your way up the system. The point is, you need to drive home one concept: you're on the brink of declaring bankruptcy but you prefer to avoid it at all costs. Tell them you're taking a loan from your in-laws, or cashing in your 401(k), or whatever other tale you need to think up to get them to believe that you're coming up with everything you potentially can and this is the best they can hope for as the alternative is likely nothing following a discharge of the debt in bankruptcy court. If you are able to convince them of that, you've a very good chance at reaching a credit card debt settlement agreement.

There are hearty costs to a charge card debt settlement agreement and it comes in the form of exceedingly bad marks on your credit score. If you're already missing payments, however, this is unlikely to do any extra damage in a practical sense as you aren't going to find individuals that are willing to loan you money with past due accounts – at least not at a fair interest rate, anyhow.

The bottom line is that a credit card debt settlement agreement may be an effective way for you to avoid bankruptcy court, the credit card company to regain some of their money, and both parties to start rebuilding the damage done to their balance sheet and earnings report from the fiasco. Likely, the biggest thing stopping you from considering it, if you're truly desperate to get in control of your finances, is pride. It's not worth it. Suck it up, take the temporary pain, and start getting your fiscal life back on track. There's a large minority of Americans that lives free from credit card debt – there's no reason you can't be among them.

As a last resort... there is bankruptcy:

In a lot of cases, it is possible to totally blot out credit card debt with a bankruptcy filing, or at the very least have a court-ordered restructuring of debt that gives you breathing space to repay your balances and get your life back in order. The opportunity price of such a move is that your credit will be totally destroyed for up to 10 years with most of the legal injury taken away after 7 years.

For a few, bankruptcy truly is the best and most efficient alternative for getting rid of credit card debt. It allows you to begin over, almost like hitting "reset" on a computer game. One of the drawbacks to think about is that the bankruptcy rules that were put in place by the credit card lobby during the Bush administration may force a lot of middle or working-class workers to file Chapter 13 (reorganization where you pay off the debt from future net income) rather than Chapter 7 (liquidation where the debts are wiped out totally). United States Congress is currently working on laws to alter this and there have been some changes already.

Intelligent credit card companies understand this. That's why it is sometimes possible to get them to drastically lower your rate of interest merely by explaining to them that you would like to repay your debt but unless the current terms are altered, you see no choice but to declare bankruptcy. You might have to stay on the telephone for 3 or 4 hours, and keep escalating from supervisor to supervisor, but at the close of the day, you have a really, very good chance of breaking down from thirty percent interest to thirteen percent interest.

If you are emotionally depleted, want to begin over, and are willing to go through the process of bankruptcy, look for a highly regarded, specified bankruptcy attorney in your area. They are able to explain all the drawbacks, expenditures, advantages, and procedures to you. In a lot of cases, it's better to just begin over and start reconstructing your life.

Chapter 8:

In 1996, 4 Israeli men, 2 of whom didn't even finish senior high, dreamed up a communication system called ICQ (I Seek YOU).

After their ground forces service, the 4 men took jobs at a local PC store. At night, they worked at their dream project....a program for blink of an eye easy net communication. They named their company Mirabilis.

Net service was really expensive in Israel, so the men moved to California and later to Greater New York. It took less than eighteen months for more than ten million PC users to download and install ICQ. ICQ was free of charge.

Those ten million individuals had heard about ICQ by "word-of-mouse" advertisement. (What we call Viral marketing or Buzz marketing). Mirabilis stated a solid 'NO" to Microsoft, but accepted a three hundred million dollar take over from AOL. ICQ then swiftly exploded to 100-million downloads and 1,000,000 fresh subscribers every week.

The interesting principle about ICQ is their marketing. They simply didn't do any marketing. All of their efforts were directed at inspiring users to spread the word.

One Way to Do It

They made it simple to spread the word by utilizing the standard e-mail that will ask your friends to join, but the software may likewise be instructed to scan your address book and send all your acquaintances invitation letters. Their thought was to construct a tool that includes an inherent mechanism for circulating the work and then simply letting it grow!

Now, to the meat and potatoes – You might not produce a program like Hotmail or ICQ but your products may go viral, bringing in tons of subscribers and revenue.

Fasten your seatbelts as you're about to learn how. How may e-books be utilized as a tool for viral marketing? Let's suppose that you sell products utilized in baking. If on your site you provide a free of charge download of an e-book with recipes that require ingredients you sell, it's conceivable that you'll sell more of the products that you manufacture. That's the primary concept but there are a lot of ways that e-books may help acquire free viral marketing for you.

If the free of charge eBook you give away on your web site is great, informative, funny, or incorporates timely info, the public will pass that info along to their friends and loved ones and thereby, yield a lot more traffic on your web site.

The cost of an eBook is just about zilch, which makes it a pretty magnetic tool for marketers big and small. The only cost is in time and creative thinking and the advantages are endless.

Naturally, eBooks don't have to be exempt. They may likewise be sold. The trick to selling your e-books is to be sure that they're worth the price you charge for them.

Many eBooks now come in PDF format, as you are able to really easily and quickly convert a text document to the PDF format. The document need not be produced in HTML first.

You are able to have images and hyperlinks to web pages in a PDF e-book. Among the greatest benefits is that the PDF format may be read by both windows and MAC users.

Using Your E-mails

Everybody wishes his or her marketing message to be viral, or have a viral facet and make the best of viral marketing. Why not? It's free of charge and effective. The issue is that most individuals don't comprehend what it is that makes their marketing e-mail message worthy of being passed along.

The idea of building an ad in email become viral is really pretty simple. You place something in there that individuals will wish to share with their loved ones and acquaintances, something they'll wish to spread around.

The messages have to be perceived as having value. Crucial or timely info, research or studies are illustrations of content that might be viewed as likely pass-along stuff. Interaction content like quizzes or personality tests are things that do get passed along, as they're entertaining.

Multimedia experiences get passed along. Rich media e-mail is getting a lot of press of late. Individuals, me included, are forever touting the advantages. Yes, it does require a bit more time and revenue investment but the messages have a excellent appeal and they do get shared with other people.... which is the aim of viral advertising.

Relevant info, research, or studies are all instances of content that might be viewed as possible pass-along stuff. Interaction material like a quiz or test can motivate a recipient to forward an e-mail... particularly if it is fun.

Getting recipients of your viral advertising e-mail to send it on to their acquaintances and colleagues isn't as difficult as it sounds. The whole trick is to make them wish to share it and thereby share your ad.

Word of advice: regardless how superb you craft the offer and regardless how great the message, if the buyer visits your web site and has an experience less than what was promised, it will return to bite you. Among the greatest things about the net is that individuals who are interested in a specific subject may come together in one tiny corner of it to share ideas and info and product reviews with each other as a niche community.

Your site has to have excellent content that's centered directly at these niche markets. Rather than selling to the masses, you sell to the individuals who are thirsty for info and resources concerning their particular interest and are most likely to buy your products or services.

To achieve this, you have to identify yourself as an authority in the field you're targeting. How does one accomplish that, you might ask.

Well, the way you prove your expertise online is by putting up on your internet site with great original and useful content.

The net delivers pictures, music and video...we all recognize that...but the most effective way to lend information is, always has been and always will be, text.

Consequently, articles are the most beneficial vehicle. If you are a great author, then you have it made...if you aren't an excellent writer, there's still a way to accomplish the goal.

There are a lot of excellent places to discover content online to add to your site and you are able to get the material free, which makes it even better. For instance, article directories. The articles are free for the taking with a condition that if you display one on your site, you have to likewise cite the article's writer and link to his or her site.

Some Practical Ways to Go Viral

When you're seeking excellent content for your niche site, you're commonly seeking articles that are well-written and bear timely info.

The 1st option, as brought up earlier, is the article directories. The articles are free of charge but you're required to link your web site to the author's web site. So 'free of charge' isn't precisely free of charge.

The 2nd option: You want articles ghostwritten for you and the way to get them is to go to article brokers. Google "Niche Article Brokers" and you'll get a lot of hits.

These companies deal with private label articles. It's content that you are able to claim as your own as all rights to the article have been sold by the writer. Now, instead of advertising somebody else as the authority, you've just demonstrated to your buyers that you, yourself, are the learned one!

You wish to make the most of the traffic you're getting on your site. So why not see to it that each visitor to your site is provided a free subscription to your e-zine within moments of getting in?

Some Tips

E-zines are a perfect illustration of informational marketing. You're presenting something of value for nothing. That value may be hard-to-find knowledge or it may be yourself.

A compelling e-zine offer matched with a easy "pass it on" technique like this won't only allow you to squeeze the most value out of each visitor to your site, but likewise give you an opt-in list of targeted leads ready and waiting to buy from you!

One of the successful attributes of a site is to maintain an e-zine by which you are able to keep in contact with your web visitors in order to maintain a reliable and long-term relationship with them through your regular e-mail to that opt-in subscriber base.

Next up, you'll discover an engaging and fun way to reach out to individuals utilizing one of the most unlikely tools around: Games.

If you've ever obtained an e-mail from a acquaintance with a link to an interesting or intriguing game, you're part of the growing target list for viral games, an net marketing tool which counts on users sending a URL to others in order to promote and theme, product or company.

Viral movies or images may be great and really funny but individuals will view them once or twice and that's it. If you are able to discover a concept that's easy to grasp, make it enjoyable and incredibly simple to utilize and then get your user to keep returning for more, you'll have the chance of exposing them a greater number of times to your message.

If you are able to add something as easy as keeping score to make a game competitive you are able to get individuals to play again and again. Offbeat games have the same effect.

The initial cost of producing a viral game is more than other viral marketing techniques but, compared to print campaigns, purchasing advertising space, radio or TV adverts, viral games are a pretty cost-efficient way of handing your market.

The other thing about games, which is difficult to put a price on, is that you are able to reach your target audience with material that's relevant and intriguing to them with ease and, once the game is set in motion, with very little work.

Although connection speed was a problem, the spread of broadband connection is slowly getting rid of that issue. There's great potential for games as a viral tool, all the same, if you're a small business, it would be best to outsource this to designers.

Viral marketing is plainly making use of the tendency of an individual to share something they find enlightening, entertaining and amazing and blogging is among the ways that viral marketing is facilitated.

These days, everyone is blogging and you are able to incorporate blogging into your sales marketing and have a lot more success.

It isn't that difficult to accomplish. Simply have your clients write diary entries about goals they've reached utilizing your product, the great emotions it's given them, the concerns and worries your product has taken out of their lives, how bad their lives were prior to them buying it, how it's helped others in their lives, how much better their lives are since they started utilizing your product, and on and on.

Clients could update their blog daily, weekly or monthly. It will hinge upon how frequently they use your product. If you're teaching them a skill, they may blog their progress.

You have to provide your buyers with web space for writing their online diary (blog) or have them e-mail you the blog entries for you to publish.

Your online blogs may be made extra persuasive by buyers including personal profiles, pictures, net video of them utilizing your product, net audio of them discussing your product, and so on.

A net blog would likely outsell the common testimonial as it's updated on a steady basis and gives more personal info and since a diary (blog) is considered private, it makes individuals more curious to read it and trust that what is said is true.

Tagging and Scripts

A Fresh consumer phenomenon is known as "tagging" or "folksonomies" (short for folks and taxonomy). Tagging is mighty because consumers are producing an organizational structure for net content. Folksonomies not only enable individuals to file away content under tags, but, even greater, share it with other people by filing it under a global taxonomy that they produced.

Here's how tagging works: utilizing sites such as del.icio.us - a bookmark sharing web site – and Flickr - a photograph sharing web site - consumers are getting together on categorizing net content under particular keywords, or tags.

For example, a person may post photos of their iPod on Flickr and file it under the tag "iPod". These pictures are now not only visible
Below the individual user's iPod tag but likewise under the community iPod tag that shows all images consumers are rendering and filing under the keyword.

Tagging is catching on, as it's a natural complement to search. Type the word "blogs" into Google and it can't tell if you're searching for info about how to launch a blog, how to read blogs, or anything else.

While tags are far from perfect, marketers ought to, all the same, be utilizing them to keep a finger on the pulse of the general public.

Begin subscribing to RSS feeds to monitor how consumers are tagging info related to your product, service, and company or web space. These are living focus groups that are available free of charge, day in and day out.

One technique of viral marketing is utilizing tell-a-friend script on your site. This is a simple computer programming script that you are able to attach to the programming on your web site.

Commonly tell a friend scripts are installed in pages where media is posted so that an individual may easily send the media to any of his acquaintances or loved ones and accomplish it swiftly.

Essentially the tell a friend script is a script where a individual may input his name, e-mail address, the recipient's e-mail address and send off the media to his acquaintance or loved ones much like an e-mail with an attachment.

Once the recipient gets the e-mail, he won't think of it as spam mail as he sees the senders name as somebody he recognizes and trusts.

Once the e-mail is opened, it will be read, watched or played. Included in the e-mail would be a short description of the company or web site that sponsors the media sent and a different tell a friend script. Then the procedure starts once more.

Tell a friend script is really easy and does not require a complicated method of programming. You'll be able to simply copy and paste a script and merely put it on a designated page.

Utilize your favorite search engine and type in "tell a friend script". There will be a lot of results. There are free of charge ones and paid ones. You simply utilize the one that best fits your needs.

By utilizing tell a friend script, you are able to possibly drive traffic into your web site and that may spell profits.

Conclusion

Divine Wealth Strategies

Success falls short when there are no good habits formed. Affirmation helps the individual to support itself towards achieving the goal because of the good habits it promotes along the way in order to keep the goal "alive". Creating and keeping good habits through daily affirmation empowers the success of the individual and the goal.

Falling short several times is not unusual when pursuing a goal. However, without proper positive affirmation it is unlikely the individual would be able to rise to the occasion by tapping into the unknown reserve powers every individual has.

Lightning Source UK Ltd.
Milton Keynes UK
UKHW050306020822
406679UK00002B/66